Are you ready for an Art Attack?

Join me on a journey around the world!

I'll show you how to get globetrotting with papier maché, household junk and just a few craft essentials.
Follow the easy steps to create the many wonders of the world in your own home! So pack your suitcase, put on your shades and let's have an

Art Attack!

D1628651

CONTENTS

700031744099

Editor: Kate Tompsett
Designer: Charlotte Reilly
Artists: Mary Hall and Paul Gamble
Model Maker: Kate Tompsett

UP, UP AND AWAY!

START YOUR ROUND-THE-WORLD TRIP IN STYLE WITH THIS BRILLIANT HOT AIR BALLOON!

1 Blow up the balloon. Stand it in a bowl, then cover it with three layers of papier maché. Leave it to dry, then pop the balloon.

2 Glue six wide strips of card to the balloon and add another layer of papier maché over the top.

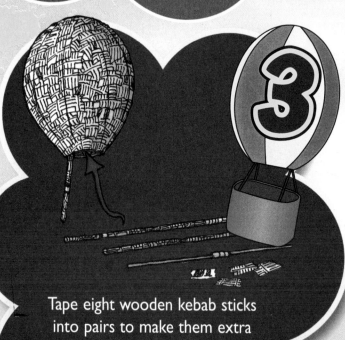

3 Tape eight wooden kebab sticks into pairs to make them extra long. Cover them with a layer of papier maché and glue them inside the balloon.

4 Cut an oval of card and tape a strip of card around it to make the basket.

Treat your toys to the trip of a lifetime!

Make a hole in the top of the balloon, thread a piece of string through it and tie a knot in the end so you can hang your balloon from the ceiling. Glue the other ends of the sticks inside the basket.

Paint the balloon with bright colours and the basket light brown with dark brown markings. Make sand bags by wrapping cotton wool balls in squares of brown fabric and tying them with string, then glue them around the edge of the basket.

CROSS THE CHANNEL WITH THIS LANDMARK NOTE-HOLDER!

1 To make Big Ben, tape a small, square box to the end of a long, narrow box. Cut four identical rectangles and snip the corners off at both ends. Tape them together in a row, then tape the ends together. Tape this shape on top of the square box. Make the pointed roof by taping four triangles together, then tape or glue a tiny card triangle to each corner, as shown.

2 To make the Eiffel Tower, start by cutting four slanted rectangles from card. Tape them together as shown, then tape two small squares of card on top and add a thin piece of cardboard for the mast. Tape another square of card to the bottom, followed by four card legs. Tape another square underneath these legs. Finally, add four slanted rectangles with an arch shape cut from each one at the bottom.

3 Cover both buildings with two layers of papier maché and leave them to dry.

4 Fold a large piece of card in half and fix triangles of card onto the corners with sticky tape. This will hold it in an upright position. Cover it with a layer of papier maché and leave it to dry.

YOU WILL NEED:

Thick card, pencil, safety scissors, sticky tape, PVA glue, newspaper, paints, paintbrush, string, mini clothes pegs.

5 Paint Big Ben and the Eiffel Tower. When they are dry, glue them to the background then glue two lengths of string between the buildings. Leave the glue to dry before pegging your notes onto the string.

GET AN "EIFFEL" OF THIS !
WHAT A CLEVER WAY TO DISPLAY YOUR NOTES!

Happy Birthday

WILD BIRTHDAY

Dear Zoe,

Thanks for inviting me to your party, I'd love to come!

Love from Julie xxx

GOING DUTCH!

MAKING THIS SIMPLE WINDMILL IS PLAIN SAILING!

1 Cut an arch shape from a piece of thick white card. Use this piece as a template to draw around, then cut out a second arch shape.

2 Cut a long strip of card and tape it around the edge of one of the shapes, fixing the sticky tape to the inside. Ask an adult to help you make a hole in the middle with a sharp pencil, pushing it through the card into a ball of modelling clay.

4 To make the sails, cut two thin strips of card and glue them together in a cross. Tape a rectangle of card onto each section and push a paper fastener through the middle.

3 Attach the sails to the windmill using the paper fastener. Fix the second cardboard arch onto the back of the windmill, putting the tape on the inside of the windmill.

5 Glue the windmill onto a square of card to make a base. Paint the base green and add details to the windmill with a marker pen.

YOU WILL NEED:

Thick white card, safety scissors, pencil, sticky tape, PVA glue, paper fastener, modelling clay, paints, paintbrush, black marker pen.

YOU COULD PUT SOMETHING HEAVY INSIDE AND USE IT AS A DOORSTOP!

FiERY FUN!

THIS TRADITIONAL CHINESE DRAGON PUPPET IS SURE TO BE A ROARING SUCCESS!

YOU WILL NEED

Thick card, pencil, safety scissors, newspaper, sticky tape, PVA glue, two wooden sticks, paints, paintbrush, yellow and blue felt.

1

Draw the shape of the dragon's head and lower jaw onto thick card and cut them out. Scrunch up some newspaper into balls and tape these in place to pad out each piece.

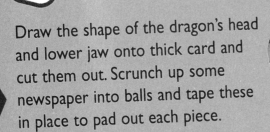

2

Add balls of newspaper to the head for eyes, with strips of newspaper over the tops to make eyelids. Bend two more strips of newspaper and fix them in place as nostrils. Draw a tongue onto card and cut it out, then fix the head and jaw together with the tongue in between.

3

Cut a strip of thin card long enough to go around the back of the head. Cut triangles from one edge to make uneven points and tape it in place. Tape on some some cardboard ears. Roll another piece of card into a cone to make the tail and cut out four legs.

4

Cover the head, legs and tail with two layers of papier maché and leave them to dry. Push one of the wooden sticks into the head and one into the tail.

5

Paint the head, tail and legs with bright colours.

6

Glue one end of the yellow felt fabric inside the head and the other end over the top of the tail.
I used fabric paint to add scales to the felt, but you could use different coloured pieces of felt.

7

Glue the legs onto the body. Cut some blue felt fabric spines and glue them onto the dragon's back.

BASKET CASE!

MAKE MESS HISS-TORY WITH THIS SNAKE CHARMER SOCK-STORER!

1 Paint a layer of PVA glue over the outside of the flowerpot and wrap the rope around it. Use sticky tape at the start and finish to hold it in place as it dries.

2 Take a second piece of rope and wrap it around itself until it is big enough to go on top of the flowerpot. Brush glue over it as you go and add a card handle to the top.

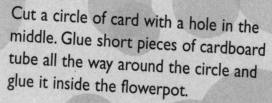

3 Cut a circle of card with a hole in the middle. Glue short pieces of cardboard tube all the way around the circle and glue it inside the flowerpot.

4 Roll up a piece of kitchen paper until it is quite thick. Pad out one end to make the snake's head.

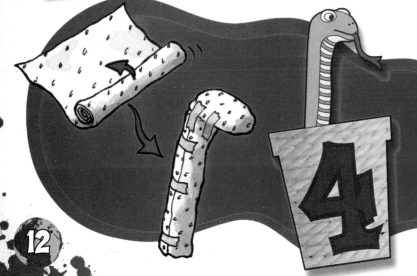

Add two balls of paper for the snake's eyes and cover him with a layer of papier maché.

5

YOU WILL NEED:
Large plastic flowerpot, rope, PVA glue, safety scissors, thin card, cardboard tubes, kitchen paper, sticky tape, newspaper, paints, paintbrush, strong thread.

Paint the snake (and the basket if you like). Glue one end of a piece of thread to the snake's head and the other end to the lid of the basket. Put the snake inside the basket and he will pop up as you lift the lid!

6

NOW SIMPLY ROLL UP YOUR SOCKS AND STORE THEM INSIDE THE CARDBOARD TUBES!

13

A PRICKLY SUBJECT!

USE THIS CACTUS PINBOARD TO DISPLAY ALL YOUR IMPORTANT MEMOS!

HOMEWORK ☺
* Maths
* Geography
* START SCIENCE PROJECT !!

THIS WEEK...
* Set video for revision programme
* Take library books back
* Cinema with Lucy?

NEXT WEEK...
@ Dentist - Monday 3-30pm
@ Gran's Birthday
@ Art Attack magazine on sale - YAY!

DON'T FORGET!
* Non-uniform day - 22nd June
* Fairy cake ingredients

YOU WILL NEED

Thick card, safety scissors, wadding (from a craft or fabric shop), PVA glue, brown, light green and dark green felt paints, paintbrush, pins

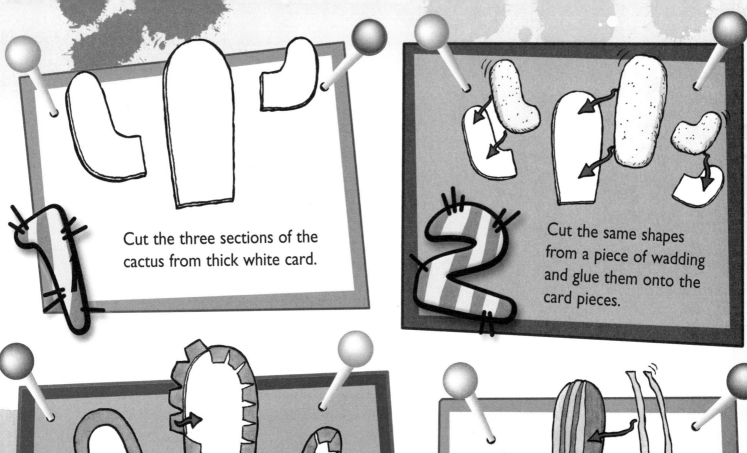

Cut the three sections of the cactus from thick white card.

Cut the same shapes from a piece of wadding and glue them onto the card pieces.

Cut pieces of dark green felt slightly bigger than the cactus shapes. Cut snips all the way around the edges, then fold them over and glue them to the back of the cactus pieces to make a neat finish.

Cut stripes from light green felt and glue them onto the cactus.

Make a pot by covering pieces of card in brown felt. Paint a background onto a large piece of card and add strips of white card to make it look like a window frame. Glue the pot in place.

Glue the cactus onto the background. Push pins into the cactus and use them to hold notes.

HELLO DOLLY!

YOU'LL HAVE STACKS OF FUN MAKING THESE CUTE RUSSIAN DOLLS!

1 Partly blow up two of the balloons so one is slightly larger than the other. Cover them with three layers of papier maché and leave them to dry, then pop the balloons.

2 Tape the two balloons together. Wrap a piece of kitchen paper around the join and add another layer of papier maché. Leave it until it's completely dry. Repeat these steps to make two more dolls, making them larger each time so they will fit inside each other. Add a disc of card to the bottom of the largest doll to stop it falling over.

Paint the dolls. Traditionally Russian dolls are dark colours, such as red, green and purple, but you can use any colours you like.

Ask an adult to help you cut the two largest dolls in half. Now you can hide them away inside each other!

COPY THESE TRADITIONAL DESIGNS OR PAINT SOME DOLLS TO LOOK LIKE YOUR FRIENDS AND FAMILY!

NOW AND ZEN!

MAKE A MINI JAPANESE GARDEN, COMPLETE WITH BLOSSOM TREES, A TEMPLE AND STATUE!

1

To make the base board, cut two identical rectangles of card. Cut a hole in the middle of one to make the lake. Paint this piece green.

2

Glue a piece of blue paper to the other rectangle of card, then stick the green piece of card on top.

STICK ON SMALL PIECES OF MOSS TO LOOK LIKE HEDGES!

YOU WILL NEED:

Thick card, safety scissors, paints, paintbrush, blue paper, PVA glue, brown craft foam, two small cardboard boxes, thin card, sticky tape, sand, small pebbles, modelling clay (the kind you bake in the oven), cocktail stick, white and green felt, pipe cleaners, tissue paper.

3 Cut strips of brown craft foam to make the path. Cut another piece and bend it to make the bridge over the lake.

TRANQUIL TEMPLE

Use two small cardboard boxes to make the temple. Make the roof by taping two card triangles onto two card rectangles. Add strips of card around the edges, then paint it as shown.

To make the sand garden, tape four strips of card into a rectangle and paint them, then fill this with sand and pebbles. Tape small pieces of card together to make the mini rake, then paint it black.

SMALL SANDPIT

SERENE STATUE

The statue is made from grey modelling clay. Roll a round head, an oval body, two arms and two legs. Flatten a piece of clay onto his head and put a blob of clay on top to make his hair. Add a small triangle of clay for his nose and use a cocktail stick to add the details to his face. Ask an adult to bake the statue for you, following the instructions on the packet.

LOVELY LILIES

Make water lilies from scraps of white and green felt.

BEAUTIFUL BLOSSOM

Twist black pipe cleaners together to make the trees, then glue on pink and white tissue paper flowers.

NEW YORK, NEW YORK!

THEY SKYLINE'S THE LIMIT WITH THIS GLITTERY AMERICAN ART ATTACK!

1 Cover the bottom half of a piece of black card with a piece of newspaper. Dip an old toothbrush into some yellow paint. Point the head of the brush downwards and use your thumb to flick the paint onto the paper. Leave it to dry.

2 Rinse out the toothbrush and use it to scrape a little blue paint along the bottom half of the picture to look like water.

3 Make the fireworks by squirting PVA glue directly onto the sky in splatter shapes. Sprinkle glitter over them and tap off the excess.

4 Add blobs of glue to the surface of the water and cover these with glitter too. Make these look more blurred than the fireworks in the sky to show they are reflections.

5 Cut a strip of black card to look like buildings. Use a gold pen to add windows and other details to them. Glue the strip along the centre of the picture.

YOU WILL NEED:

Black card, yellow, blue and black paint, glitter, gold pen, PVA glue, safety scissors, old toothbrush.

6 Cut a moon from card and use the gold pen to colour it in.

7 Add the buildings' reflections with black paint and a reflection of the moon with gold pen.

PERFECT PYRAMID!

STORE YOUR ART MATERIALS IN THIS EGYPTIAN-THEMED BOX

1 Cut a triangle from a piece of strong white card. The triangle needs to be equilateral; the same length on each side. Draw around it and cut it out three more times. Cut a large square of card to make the base.

2 Paint the base board yellow and add Egyptian designs with felt-tip pens.

3 Cut one of the triangles in half as shown. Cut the other three large triangles in the same way.

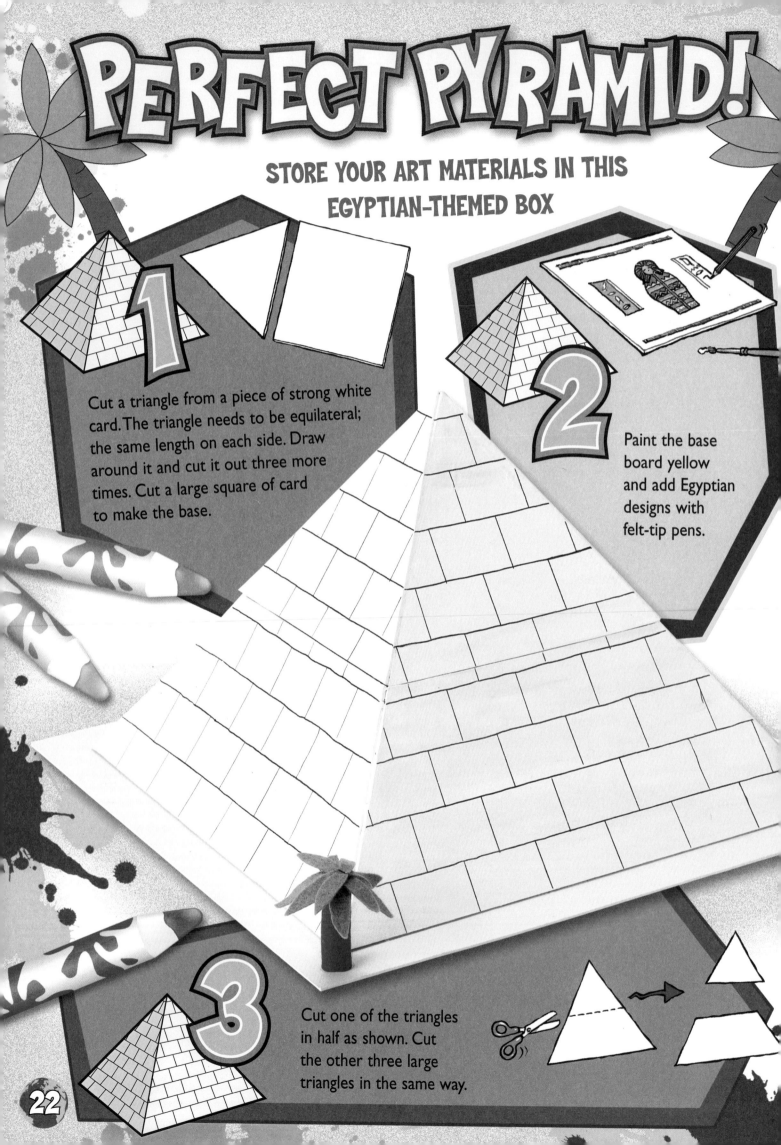

LOOK FOR ANCIENT EGYPTIAN DESIGNS IN BOOKS OR ON THE INTERNET

YOU WILL NEED:

Strong white card, safety scissors, pencil, PVA glue, sticky tape, paints, paintbrush, felt-tip pens, marker pen, brown and green felt.

Tape the four small triangles together in a row and fold them around to make a pyramid shape. Stick them together with the sticky tape on the inside. Tape the other pieces of card into a row in the same way to form the lower half of the pyramid.

4

Glue the bottom half of the pyramid onto the base. Paint both parts of the pyramid yellow and leave them to dry, then add details with a thin black marker pen.

5

To make the palm trees, roll up small pieces of brown felt and glue green felt leaves to the tops.

6

ALL ABOARD!

MAKE THIS BRILLIANT BUS FRAME AND TAKE YOUR FRIENDS ON AN AMAZING JOURNEY!

YOU WILL NEED:
Thin card, safety scissors, glue, felt-tip pens, photographs.

1 Trace or photocopy the bus on the opposite page onto thin card. Colour it in. Don't forget to add your destination to the front of the bus!

3 Cut slots at the bottom of each of the windows and tuck your passengers into place. Use glue to hold them in place permanently, or leave them loose so you can change them whenever you like!

2 Cut passengers from photographs. You can use photos of your friends or family, or cut out pictures of your favourite stars from a magazine.

ART 28 CHARING CROSS ATTACK

24

GIVE US A WAVE!

MAKE FUNKY FLAGS FROM SIMPLE FELT SHAPES!

YOU WILL NEED: Felt in different colours, string, safety scissors, glue, star sequins.

Glue seven thin strips of red felt onto a white rectangle to make the American flag. Add a small blue rectangle to the top left-hand corner and cover it with silver star sequins.

TIP!

Cut a rectangle of paper to use as a template, to make sure all your flags are the same size.

Glue a red circle of felt onto a white background to make the Japanese flag.

Spain's flag is made from a rectangle of yellow felt, with two horizontal red stripes.

Belgium, France and Italy's flags each have three vertical stripes: black, yellow and red for Belgium; blue, white and red for France; and green, white and red for Italy.

TRY AND FIND SOME MORE DESIGNS TO COPY, OR HAVE FUN MAKING UP SOME OF YOUR OWN!

The Union Jack has a blue background with red and white diagonal stripes, finished with a large red and white cross in the middle.